COLLOQUY AT THE ABYSS:
A FUGITIVE AMALAGAM

HAROLD ABRAMOWITZ
&
WILL ALEXANDER

WITH AN INTRODUCTION
BY
RYAN IKEDA

Colloquy at the Abyss: A Fugitive Amalgam
© 2020 Harold Abramowitz, Will Alexander, Ryan Ikeda
Insert Blanc Press
ISBN: 978-1-947322-80-6

Cover and half-title page designed by Matt Normand based on a coloured pencil drawing by Will Alexander entitled *Beauty of the Answerless*, 2014.

Acknowledgements:

An audio version of the conversation appeared in the May 2016 issue of The Conversant. Thank you to the editors there. Thank you to Zachary Trent, Andy Fitch, and Ryan Ikeda for additional work on the conversation. Thank you to Ryan Ikeda for the introduction. The authors would like to thank Mathew Timmons for his work on this project.

COLLOQUY AT THE ABYSS:

A Fugitive Amalgam

Harold Abramowitz
& Will Alexander

with an introduction by Ryan Ikeda

PRESS

Los Angeles

CONTENTS

LISTENING PRACTICE: AN INTRODUCTION   7
    Ryan Ikeda

COLLOQUY AT THE ABYSS   *11*
    Will Alexander & Harold Abramowitz

AND THEN, IN HERE   *47*
    Harold Abramowitz

POEMS: INDELIBLE ROTATIONS   65
    Will Alexander
         Pre-Cognitive Volation *drawing*   *66*
         The Iridescent Enigma   *67*
         The Blood Penguin   *72*
         from Concerning the Henbane Bird   *77*
         from Exobiology As Goddess   *83*

Listening Practice: An Introduction

Ryan Ikeda

What you now hold was once a conversation between Harold Abramowitz and Will Alexander, recorded at a coffee shop somewhere in Los Angeles, and then transcribed by several listeners at various locations across the country. This book is not a book but a mediation of those sense experiences—as sound was separated from bodies and then concretized into text.

I know Harold and Will 'electronically', which is another way of saying I haven't met them in person. We have never even spoken, but I have read through their poetry and email correspondence. As one of the transcribers, I first encountered this "book" as an MP3 recording, where my role was to transfer Will and Harold's audible conversation into written form; an exchange that resembles translation.

Some have described translation as an act of necessary betrayal (*traduttore, traditore*) in which the translator must deviate from literal translation to convey the poetic moments embodied in the original tongue. For transcription, the language stays the same, but its medium changes; the shift from audio to writing affects an aesthetic re-rendering of the sense experience associated with Will and Harold's project, and changes its audience from listeners into readers. Transcription betrays the original in yet another aspect, it marks an objectification of the material substance of the project, now a book. As an object, sound becomes palpable—property not of the ears, but of the hands and the eyes. *Colloquy at The Abyss* seeks to defamiliarize sense experience in order to question the way we listen and the way public life and personal experience continuously intermingle.

*

Colloquy at The Abyss examines the common—but overlooked—aspects of hearing. Will and Harold chose a public coffee shop to record their conversation as opposed to a private residence or a recording studio. To record a conversation in public is to record the conversation *and* the public. As you experience *Colloquy at The Abyss* this becomes clear as the people and objects that pass by their table walk their way into the conversation—children standing at a stoplight, a voice recorder, newspapers piled on a table. Sound resists containment and troubles the distinction between public and private domains; *Colloquy* orients its readers to a political critique entailed by the act of listening.

The ear is always receptive to sound. Unlike the eye, the ear cannot close itself off to sensation, but remains open to its environment. Even when I stuff my ears with pink rubber foam, I am still receptive to the ambient noises outside my body—the cars speeding down the street, my wife tapping her keyboard in the next room, an upstairs neighbor urging her walker across a wooden floor. I may muffle these sounds, but I cannot stop my ears from receiving them. The ear captures sound from the body's internal biorhythms, too. In his famous attempt to hear silence, John Cage entered an acoustic chamber devoid of all external sound only to discover that its absence only emphasized the internal whir of his circulatory system pumping blood through his veins. If sound overruns spatial divisions, reveals such divisions as constructs, it does through the body. Hearing connects us to our bodies in a way that is inextricable from environment, the public forum, or the body politic, but *Colloquy* pushes this connection forward to an interrogation of our listening practices.

While we commonly correlate what we see with what is real ("seeing is believing"), linking sight to an unexamined belief, we often connect sound—through its repetition and rhythms—to memory. Ancient poetry functioned similarly, as a mnemonic structure, or storage device, for mythmaking that relied heavily upon an ear attuned to the natural rhythms of public life. In contemporary American experience, the practice of listening no longer relies on the body to store memories but external technological apparatus: now we most often encounter sound privately, through headphones, earbuds, portable speakers, or a car stereo. Our listening practices, personalized and mediated by technological devices, attenuates individual connection to the public sphere; and yet these devices afford new sound experiences. Recording devices like the iPhone, portable recorder, or the much earlier gramophone, return the white noise, ambience, non-literal experiences lost in transcription; we encounter an experience where we hear everything, not only human voices.

*

Colloquy questions the connection between sound and the production of knowledge. The digitization of sounds atomizes experience away from conscious perception such that: to record no longer signifies to remember (an act that entails consciousness and a body). Recently, my wife and I strolled around Lake Merritt. As we walked, we discussed the reliability of cloud storage as a secure means to archive papers at the Bancroft Library. As I mulled this method, I considered how quickly a digital library could be lost by an errant stroke of a key, like a "Library of Alexandria" I remarked aloud to my wife. Later, when we returned to our apartment, and I returned to transcribing Will and Harold's conversation, I heard Harold use the same phrase. Slyly, "Library of Alexandria" had crept into my mind after days of transcribing Will and Harold's conversation, lodged in my unconscious, and structured an association without leaving any trace of its origin.

*

Colloquy suggests that to listen is to remain open to the public and aware of technological mediation, which displaces the ear's sense experience by storing/producing sound via a recording device, apart from the human body. Disembodied, sound's political critique—its ability to traverse boundaries—wanes; hearing no longer reminds us of our interrelatedness to the public sphere and our environment, but reinforces a notion of private experience and a voluntary relationship to public life. *Colloquy* troubles this disconnect, what Harold calls our "incredible cosmic isolation" (24). By situating their conversation in a coffee shop, *Colloquy at The Abyss* contextualizes their conversation among a contested public space surrounded by violence:

> "When you look around the corner from here, where the robbery occurred, you're talking about this major gentrification project happening on Main Street and Broadway and over there. It's literally 50-yards away from some of the worst poverty in the world, and it's always been that way. I grew up here. You grew up here." (14)

Colloquy protests against the privatization of intellectual discourse and questions the ways in which class segregates our listening practices, granting access to some while excluding voices (as a private residence indicates) and privileging (through a recording studio) others. Sound carries thoughts across boundaries, from mind to mind, a mutual exchange of influence occurs through hearing; cultivating this sense leads to listening enough to differentiate human voices from "a series of static" (26). The ear is receptive to its environment through its embodied configuration; as earbuds replace embodied sound experience, dulled, muted, muffled, or returned as an object, *Colloquy* advocates for a quality of the ear, for its receptivity to remain open to the environment and public space; a practice of listening, or, listening practice.

Ryan Ikeda
2015

COLLOQUY AT THE ABYSS:
Harold Abramowitz & Will Alexander

Harold Abramowitz: I get very self-conscious when I know I'm being taped.

Will Alexander: This reminds me of the European 14th century, with the disparity between rich and poor, people having general paranoia.

HA: Right.

WA: With all the pollution and economic distinctions going on at the same time with the climate; it's all up for grabs.

HA: That's true.

WA: The technology is so intense and so precise, and the social structure is in such disarray—such an apocalyptic contrast.

HA: Yeah, and it seems like it's getting worse, as far as the intensity building to a breaking point, in certain ways, because it's so untenable. You can't imagine the tension lasting.

WA: I can't see this tension continuing in its constant concentration. Like a general breakdown, a mortal disease, the planet's like a diabetic having some kind of fatality brewing inside of it. If it's just a Democratic political base talking about climate change...

HA: Yeah, if they ban plastic bags in L.A. County, are they too late?

WA: It seems it's already too late. It's the mentality of materialistic consciousness that always waits until you see something you can measure—whereas an animal that's telepathic, he or she can sense an entity dwelling in the environment before there's any physical manifestation of it. This is the energy that the old tribal peoples knew. There's a certain sensitivity to the climate and the environment, not only the climate of the exterior world, but the climate in the internal world, of individuals, of nuance—a climate of nuance that has been totally misused. We dig up the earth. We just destroy to create some kind of square or a barrier, and so the concept of God has been completely squared off in a rectangle inside of an institution or a church, which is completely ridiculous. In fact, how do you account for fractals in mountain chains, if that's a part of creation, too? It's irregular. It's difficult to measure. In fact, you really don't measure all those fractal mathematics. You come up with some kind of minimum-measurement formula, and that's only very recently. That can't account for viper fish and the patterns in the Canadian Rockies. Those things are just completely spontaneous and this is something that scares the mentality in the Occident.

HA: That's right.

WA: Because it wants to contain everything and create this giant egotism.

HA: When you look around the corner from here, where the robbery occurred, you're talking about this major gentrification project happening up on Main Street and Broadway and over there. It's literally 50-yards away from some of the worst poverty in the world, and it's always been that way. I grew up here. You grew up here. It's always been that way, and it's never ever been addressed.

WA: This is a chronic problem. It's not a modern problem. It's been a chronic problem for at least 800 years—longer. We have had a social breakdown and my take on it is that we opted out at the fall of Islamic Granada. The institutions were so arranged at that time that Christians, Muslims and Jews were able to function together on major projects of thought, despite differences. In other words, there was an atmosphere of tolerance that completely broke down when the Christians took over. In fact, there were almost 600 years between the situation the Jewish population faced in Spain and in Germany, between 1348 and 1948. In 1348 there was a rumor that was sent out that the Jewish population had fostered the plague, which we know was obviously not the case. [In Germany, this population was forced to self-immolate themselves in their own homes, which happened in the 1300's during the time of the Plague.] There was no Renaissance that took place in the 1400s and 1500s (not really). In terms of architecture and painting: Leonardo da Vinci. But in terms of social structure, it never was transmuted by the Renaissance. In fact, women were being burned at the stake, the Indian extermination was transpiring, the slave trade was rising.

HA: Religious intolerance existed before being herded into various kinds of ghettos. Getting knighted, things like that…

WA: Exactly, exactly: titles and knighthood, which we see today. It's the same thing—instead of riding around in armor and a horse, they ride a Maserati. It's true.

HA: Here's a question off-the-subject: I was blown away when I was looking at *Singing in Magnetic Hoofbeat*. I didn't know that you knew Merilene Murphy. When I read the book I was very moved, because she was a good friend of mine. I had always meant to ask if you knew her.

WA: Yeah, I did know her fairly well. She was a very big supporter of mine. Beautiful person, very sincere and a lot of energy—intense energy, which you fail to see in the American poetic landscape these days. It's conservative. It seems to be more conservative and more selective, and more affluent.

HA: Well, she represented another kind of energy.

WA: Yeah. She also represented someone in the poetic landscape who was consistently nice, which can be a kind of rarity in the current landscape. She was just really nice and supportive, always a nice person, always.

HA: A very supportive individual.

WA: There are neglected ideas, neglected landscapes, neglected persons, neglected energies, which we need to bring to the foreground. We live in such a culture of fickleness that it is a continuous problem. I think someone did a study of memory patterns in 1967, and it was like the collective memory pattern was maybe a few seconds. Now it's the low minuses probably.

HA: It's true.

WA: People are just basically empty at this time, and giving back empty calories.

HA: It's incredible. My students, it's incredible, just the lack of knowledge. Not as an indicator of intelligence, very intelligent people, but zero knowledge. Literally zero knowledge, zero ability to apply any kind of knowledge to anything, which is scary.

WA: It's scary. This is a problem, because we are concerned with the memory of the race, and it seems we've been cut off from history, in general, by 1945, which is when all of us were sired. We are post-bomb people. There are very few pre-bomb people around at this time, so everybody's pretty much post-bomb, everybody. I just saw a bunch of three-year-olds crossing the street up there. We're all in the same category of being post-bomb individuals.

HA: Yeah, I saw them walking up there…

WA: Yeah, they were very cute kids, but they've been born into a situation with the background jangling. As Helen Caldicott points out, the circumstances of the nuclear have not gone away. We've just talked it out of our heads after 1990. People born into this atmosphere have lost track of the fact that these things are still here. We still have B-52s flying around. Can you imagine?

HA: Missile silos, Cold War ICBMs. I was just having a conversation with my friends, reminding myself of the tremendous culpability of Harry Truman, and the Harry Truman Administration (one of his first acts was dropping the bomb) and the

National Security Act of 1947 institutionalizing all the wartime military and intelligence—it's still there.

WA: 1945 through 1947 were very crucial years. In his recent film series, *The Untold History of the United States*, Oliver Stone brings some work out on forgotten areas of American history, and he mentions a tremendous faux pas that was made with Henry Wallace, the running-mate of Franklin Roosevelt, who was completely anti-fascist, very intelligent, and very forward-looking in terms of cleaning up the social misconstructions of American society at that time. The Democratic Party made sure that they could oust him and put in a high-school graduate, who was Harry Truman. This is the extent that these power-mongers will go to conceive or contain power within what they think is relevant. This includes assassinations, character defamation, you name it.

HA: Because right after that, it was like 1947 or 48, you have the coup in Iran. This was the first CIA…

WA: No 1953.

HA: 1953, yeah. Right in the last year Truman was president. So, that inaugurates the era of CIA operations.

WA: We're still in this. We're stuck in the situation, and this is fascinating. I heard a lady on BBC talking about Mick Jagger, and she wanted the moment to stay put, as it was.

HA: Which moment? 1975?

WA: Something like that. *Brown Sugar* or something.

HA: 1972?

WA: Something like that. She just wants that moment to stay, and this is the environment we're dealing with: the moment of psychic decay and frustration and a general juvenilia transpiring in the American psyche. I'm interested in people who seem to be pawns in circumstance. I'm trying to investigate this whole idea of power, and I'm typing up a play at the present time on Emperor Asoka, and his transition between warfare and Buddhism. He was the Mauryan Emperor. Asoka was a black ruler, the third ruler of the Mauryan Empire who, after being an incredible and supreme killer, turned away from killing and the edicts of warfare, and so this play (*At Night On The Sun*) is concerned about the adaptation of peace and the struggle that ensues when turning away from war. The play incorporates hyper-dimensional levels via partial adaptation from elements of Noh theatre. In this play I am examining his turning away from exterior power towards internal liberty. This idea of kingship is based on the Guayaki Indians of Paraguay where the king doesn't have the same power, the same inclination, say, as in an imperial orthodoxy.

HA: Right. I'm always interested when you make analogies with the Roman Empire. I think one of my favorite things that you've written was a blurb for Marcella Durand's book. And I don't remember exactly what the wording was but it was kind of—you know, the image was of the Roman enclave. Remember that?

WA: Yes I do.

HA: It reminds me of Philip K. Dick, where it's like the Empire still exists, where we're actually still walking in the Roman Empire.

WA: We still are. It's never ceased to exist—the whole idea of matter being primary and consciousness secondary, that's a big, big issue. Everything has to be materialized and possess a tremendous stature in order to be recognized. It's a spot-light consciousness and it never takes into account anything on the periphery. It's always wanting to uproot, you know, like the Roman soldiers uprooted the foundations of the Carthaginians after the Third Punic War, the after effects we are still feeling today. I still believe as did Rimbaud that using language in a certain way "is to change life," that you can change life through the use of language, because when I do yoga it is done during sleep...

HA: How long have you been doing that?

WA: For quite some time. I've noticed an interstice between initial sleep and dreaming, if I have the radio at a certain volume, a very low volume, the sound gets inside my dreams and it projects images. Hearing is the primal element, not the visual. We are totally inculcated in the idea of seeing. I guess though that's why so many poets that are practicing are completely retinally oriented rather than aurally oriented. Once you are retinally oriented, you only receive partial input energy of the soil and the oceans. In this sense one is excluded from the basic elements of real living. An optical culture tends to scale its orientation towards extrinsic value.

HA: Oh yeah.

WA: What's growing in the soil is simultaneous with the life-force instilled within us. I see this force going back to living intuition, but unfortunately we seem to be cut off from history in this era, so we just punch in inert information and think that that is enough. For instance, there exists the erosion of energy attributed to handwriting. There is growing estrangement from the process.

HA: I have always struggled with handwriting. It's always been a kind of bane for me, my poor handwriting.

WA: Poor or not, the electricity of the hand transmits the energy in your system that allows you to write something. Whereas when you punch in something on a piece of machinery, to me it cuts you off from yourself in the long run.

HA: Yeah, actually one of the things I just replaced before I met you was my notebook.

WA: Yeah, yeah.

HA: One of those things I always carry.

WA: We have been forced to depend on so many things outside of ourselves. All of our information seems to come not from inside but from outside of us, and there is a loss of wisdom and a loss of telepathy, a loss of contact with one's sensitivity.

HA: Like you said, it's a loss of hearing—it's a loss of the ability to listen.

WA: People want to see something. They don't want to listen. How does it look rather than how it is in terms of its reality. This is an interesting situation, so you know they say an intelligent seven-year-old could shut this whole system down, you know, by just punching a few buttons. And this is…

HA: Totally compromised.

WA: Well this stuff is compromised. I remember walking into a bank one day and the system went down and people were panicking. I said "Just write it down."

HA: I had that happen yesterday. I went to the DMV to replace my license and the system was down. I have to go back Monday.

WA: The system is down, you know? I was told all this information has to be centered in one particular place.

HA: Right.

WA: And that's dangerous, but I mean they have cables running from America toward North Africa, wherever. And when one of those cables goes down with all the information on it, what happens—it goes haywire. And it's that whole idea of basing everything in one packet, so one can know where it is.

HA: We get the Library of Alexandria syndrome.

WA: Yes, exactly. This is not safe, and the only people who seem to be taking action are on the outskirts: indigenous individuals in Canada, in the Southwest, fighting the pipelines and the irrigation disaster that's going on. We are right on the verge of something that I find analogous to the situation in New York, which happened a few days ago, when the apartment complex blew up and that gas had been going for days and no one bothered to deal with it. It's kind of like a climate going up. People announce it and do reports on it and there's no action on it.

HA: Yeah, I'm actually surprised it doesn't happen more often. It's something I've always been paranoid about.

WA: Oh of course, yes.

HA: In particular in New York. New York has pipes that have not been replaced since the 1890s.

WA: New York is quite vulnerable. Its infrastructure is structured in such a way that you really can't do much about it because there is so much activity. In other words, it's the American psyche. They can't really shut anything down. People are so wired up doing something all the time that they would go nuts. And this whole idea of money coming through all the time and finances and just this and that—how come you can't just shut something down and repair it? Your body has to shut down to sleep. That is when it repairs itself.

HA: Yeah, retire something gracefully, you know?

WA: Exactly.

HA: Retire something gracefully, like the horse or something. You know it has done its service to humanity, so then let it go.

WA: Let it go and go graze.

HA: But it can't be done. It still has its equestrian shows, service, this kind of extraneous…

WA: Just busy work. Everybody wants to be busy, which is not a good thing all the time. There is an old Aldous Huxley novel, *Antic Hay*, that speaks to this whole idea of continuing to keep busy. And this is basically the idea of the Western person's sense of accomplishment.

HA: Right.

WA: Not that he or she is continuously doing something that is completely relevant, but he or she is just doing something.

HA: That's right.

WA: No imagination can transpire in that kind of context whatsoever. What Charles Fourier was talking about was this utopianism where you only have to work for so long and then let the imagination take over. And the American Indians would do that and then, when they were invaded, people wanted them to work all the time.

HA: Right.

WA: They had resting points, you know: you work then you rest then you work then you rest, but here everything has to be continuously, you know, steady. Then you get that glassy-eyed feeling of people who need psychological sleep.

HA: Well first of all, it's the same thing, the inability to understand when to stop, when to cease. Then it turns into this constant state of dissociation. It's like the chaos of constant dissociation.

WA: Constant dissociation in the sense of fatigue all the time. You get into medical territory, Ambien and Humira and all of these—with half of the advertising based on the fact that this particular thing can kill you, rather than help you. The trace amounts help you live without rheumatism, but at the same time the majority activity of this medicine will, in the long-term, exterminate you. This is the whole idea of "just do it": just bulldoze it, blow it up, invade it, invade it, invade it. We invade our bodies, the universe. This is my problem, too, with space exploration. When you go to Europa, are you going to implant some type of social system that is based on this?

HA: The answer is yes.

WA: Yes. They would. I don't find the Occident to be very advanced at all. There is an African-American psychologist, Na'im Akbar, who talks about this. The circumstance in the West is completely backwards. The technology may have reached a certain kind of acme, but the social conditions that produce this type of acme are completely flawed and oblivious, because they are suicidal. We're living on everything that's based on a suicide. I sometimes feel like I'm walking around millions of suicides every day. And people are oblivious. They say it's normal. It's like the normality of living in Jonestown every day. I hate to say this, but it's so scary.

HA: Look at the situation in the Pacific Ocean, this constant drawing from the source and drawing from the source without any kind of consciousness of replenishing or acknowledging that you're actually taking something.

WA: Seafood restaurants: it's just fish, fish, fish, fish, with no letting the ocean replenish itself. And we have this situation continuously going on all the time. Right now, we have the problem of Fukushima with tons of cesium going out (I want to say 3 tons of water a day, an amazing amount of bad waters coming out of those Fukushima complexes daily, pouring straight into the Pacific) and Abè now wants to continue nuclear proliferation, in terms of more power plants, which is absolutely insane.

HA: It was insane from day one.

WA: From day one. This is a compound complex circumstance: people running around voting for him, working with the situation as if normal, but we know right now that it may be some kind of disaster where, long term, some form of evacuation may directly effect the population of Tokyo.

HA: The point is that no one knows how to fix it.

WA: This is the insanity of our general circumstance: we have nowhere to go. In spite of space exploration and the cosmos and post-Carl Sagan, where do you put large populations in terms of interstellar space? Or even small ones? Maybe we shouldn't even talk about it with such definitive projection, but it seems such a scenario is just around the corner.

HA: We can talk about it since we're in Space Shuttle Square.

WA: We are in Space Shuttle Square, so we can talk about that. In other words, there's no place to go. Interstellar space is daunting, is daunting, uncountable galaxies, uncountable planets, uncountable terms. This is like a situation in the...

HA: Incredible cosmic isolation.

WA: We are cosmically isolated. It's no better than Copernicus. We're beholden to this planet, psychologically, and we are beholden to these ghettos. And when I say this, I mean Beverly Hills, the Hamptons, North Philly, Watts—these are isolated areas condensed according to fear. A situation not unlike the psyche of the English peasant circa 1356. Everything is fear. Everything is outside yourself and you have nothing inside of yourself. At that time it was so bad that at least in those areas you could say, "Well, it's the church, it's this, it's that." At this time we don't know where anything is really coming from. You really don't. It's the corporations. It's the presidency. We don't know. Quite honestly we don't know where it is, and I don't think they know either. I don't think anyone knows.

HA: I think the so-called financial crisis from a few years ago illustrated that, with the "too big to fail" idea, where we have structures that we can't let fail because we don't actually know what they do. We can't actually articulate the ways in which they are wired into everything. So the fear is: we take that away, we actually don't know…

WA: We don't know what we have. All we know is we don't know where we're going. And because this is here it gives us some kind of marker in a forest in which we're lost. So it's a negative familiarity, and we're working on these tense negatives all the time. It's always a negative. Everybody's looking over their shoulders. Everybody's paranoid. Like for the CIA's spying on Diane Feinstein, it was OK with the NSA doing it to everyone else, but when it happened to her, she was quite…

HA: It was a constitutional crisis.

WA: Yeah. Shows you the idea, the isolation of people in the Senate, Congress. They have no idea what's going on in the rest of the world. If they do, it's like John McCain who wants to go over and be forceful with Russia. It's completely stupid because he knows that it's just rhetoric. You know, if you send an American army over there what are you going to get?

HA: And a big chunk of the former Soviet Union's nuclear arsenal was in the Ukraine, which is always a sensitive area.

WA: By doing that, you are putting the American people at risk rather than reducing the risk. This is the kind of insane rhetoric we have going on at the so-called "highest levels."

HA: And you're right, it's rhetoric and there is this weird kind of incantation of misunderstanding and ignorance because it resonates out into the world. Like we were saying before, people don't have the skills to process rhetoric as rhetoric and, instead, perceive all kinds of pronouncements as truth.

WA: What's terrifying is (following on that very crucial point you just made), I think Krishnamurti said it: if you say something over and over and over again, it seems to take on an energy of truth. It's very unfortunate, this rhetorical environment we're in. As you mentioned earlier, we still have people with no information, zero information, and you keep telling them something over and over again. I run into people that have been living on this planet for over 80 years, with a mouth full of platitudes. What would you spend your time on Earth doing? You're supposed to work on yourself. Heartbreaking thought: I see three-year-olds, I see 80-year-olds, and I see similarities there. People starting out in the same direction and people are ending in that same direction, with no intervention from any higher perspective—or their own perspective. No originality, in other words. Bottom line: you're fostering a whole population of replicators.

HA: A series of static…

WA: No alchemy, no alchemy whatsoever. Like in the southern part of this city there's not much going on. There's no energy being put over there: no restaurants have been put down there, maybe one in that whole region. And so how do you expect to create circulation and atmosphere? So we are dealing with these intense provincialisms. It's almost like the atmosphere cast by the church during the time of Bruno. Liberty was non-existent and should it have been personally evinced, it was a good chance that one would end like Bruno, charred at the stake. You know, if you cross over and find that you can look in an infinite field rather than a shallow or provincial field, and you don't have any kind of example outside of what's being told to you, it becomes a daunting circumstance. And that type of atmosphere for poets is very difficult. I think, though, in many ways, the poets get out of these provinces, psychological provinces and schools, and begin to just be free with themselves, with language, rather than look at themselves as "authors" with this and that limitation which keeps a provincial psychology intact, which only approves of a certain type of person. The imagination should be able to flow. Right now, it seems that in many ways the poetry community is behind the astronomical community in that an explorational template is being invoked thereby allowing an expansion and empowerment of its basic language.

HA: I was also reading your essay about the exploding of genre—an exploding of social genres, all of those.

WA: It's my feeling that we are at such a crucial stage, we have to share this information across-the-board, not just in our group or in terms of people that we previously wanted nothing to do with. Kind of like in a crisis, you know, when the waters are rising everybody has to throw in the sandbags. You can't worry about who's throwing the sandbags in. Let's just get the sandbags in.

HA: It is a depressing state. I mean I sometimes feel like I'm frustrated in my writing work, because I don't have a recognizable gimmick. Like in the musical *Gypsy*: "You gotta have a gimmick." It's frustrating because it's hard to have a certain kind of traction without it.

WA: Of course.

HA: I think, "OK, if I were working as a poet with traction and a writer with traction in that way, then I should be marketing my daily life—no way!"

WA: No. I mean we are in a gimmick-laden circumstance. The people who interview poets in the media, even the so-called progressive media, do not get it right. They do not get it right. They are interviewing people who seem to be commodities of the moment. In other words it fits in a niche. You become recognized for a gimmick. You're not recognized for a living language, which is a language ultimately anonymous, without authorship. It should be based on the essence of what the person has said, not on his or her demographic, or "you're this age now" or "you can wear that sweater now."

HA: It's also like a positionality based on optical apparatus. And it's the idea that, you know, one's expression, writing practice, is informed by positionality and being able to point the finger, point this kind of optical gaze, and being able to comment on it—which is the opposite of what you're saying.

WA: It's part of the commodification of language.

HA: And in that way it doesn't matter what stance or what position. You are closing yourself in.

WA: Yeah.

HA: Which I myself think comes out of fear.

WA: Fear and wanting to be included in the group. To me it's like being on the *Titanic*. Everybody wanted to be on the *Titanic*, but it sunk. In other words, to get to the deepest root of language (like the British critic Martin Seymour Smith was talking about Vallejo being the greatest poet of the 20th century because he had gotten down to this level of stuttering in the language), that pure, pure fuel, that flint where it flakes off—like Gherasim Luca the Romanian surrealist poet. At this stuttering level, this specific honesty of poetic act, where there is no gentrification of language, with all the educated footnotes and references, where a poem that has 20 lines has three pages of footnotes. That's not what we're looking for. What we're getting more and more is too much education. The writer E.M. Cioran, in an interview some years back, said that it's not good because writers know too-too much. Leave some space for the imagination to grow.

HA: Right.

WA: In other words, take a chance on something, which is not done that much. You want to have a preplanned schedule on how you are going to create, and it's not workable. And this is one thing about the life of poetry: it resists that commercialization. It doesn't work on that level. You can't tame it, like wild horses and mustangs—they are out there running and they want to run. They don't want to be pinned into someone's backyard. Here we have the poem that is pinned into someone's backyard and it is nice and neat. It's technically proficient and it's intelligent. It doesn't have any power. I was looking at a piece of writing recently and I felt this metallic energy coming off of it. It is intelligent, but it is not active in terms of its conjunction point, the electricity coursing through it. Sometimes electricity is not verbally correct. I mean Faulkner was not stellar with sentence construction. He didn't need that.

HA: Right

WA: Let someone else do that. They have plenty of opportunity to do that, but we don't have many people who have the capability of an expansive imagination. We have editors, but we don't have real poets in the culture who talk about the future or the way trends are going, and, you know, this is what the poet originally would do. A vatic person could talk about the future and about things that are not seen. We now have people who want to fit in and talk about things that happened already.

HA: That's right.

WA: So it's safe. Never take chances. People praise Rimbaud, but could they take him personally if he walked in here and cursed them out?

HA: That's right.

WA: Threw over tables?

HA: The idea of being excited by wielding models that are not of your time and place—that always kind of gets me.

WA: Yes.

HA: Here's the moment. But rather than trying to figure out what's appropriate for the time and place you find yourself in, you're going to use something that has already been done.

WA: We see that.

HA: Then it's a kind of fight to the death to preserve that.

WA: This is the structure of an institutional writer, of an intelligent institutional writer.

HA: Of all stripes, as well.

WA: Of all stripes. Of all stripes. And those institutions are considered to be radical. But a lot of that stuff is codified by the culture, too, and these individuals make thousands of dollars to make speeches and talk about how they fought the system—because it's been brought into the system. So how do you keep that energy of chance alive in an atmosphere that needs it to fail, to keep its fire alive as part of one's respirational component?

HA: And also the point is that if we're on a continuum from Rome, and there was no Renaissance, then, you know, the alternative has not been found.

WA: No, it hasn't.

HA: Reviving failed models of revolution doesn't seem to make sense.

WA: No, it doesn't. It's an illusion that we had a big changeover and things are somehow better because of the Renaissance. The slave trade was just getting started. Thomas Jefferson said that black people didn't have the intelligence to write poetry. How can you go with that? Genocide in the New World. You know, the situation with Asia and the United States that Ronald Takaki addressed some years prior concerning the different types of racisms between the Indian, the Asian, and the Black people and how this is played across the 19th century. This is why, for one of my earlier books, all of my blurbs came from women.

HA: Was that *Exobiology?*

WA: No, that was *Above the Human Nerve Domain*. It was Leslie Scalapino, Harryette Mullen, Diane Ward and Norma Cole. This whole idea of not working with gender provinciality is supremely important. You have racial, gender, and class problems malignantly condensed. This is why it was important for me to collaborate with Janice Lee on *The Transparent As Witness*.

HA: Yeah, I heard about that. I haven't seen it yet.

WA: We did that collectively over a period…not long. I did another book with another writer. It was quite interesting. His name is Carlos Lara.

HA: Yeah, I know him.

WA: Yeah, Carlos. It is called *The Audiographic As Data*. It is another collective book which I actually did prior to this one. Collaborative projects with like-minded artists.

HA: I like to work collectively as well.

WA: Collective writing staunches dogmatism. It is just the way that two minds are better than one. In our commercialist onslaught all the time, how do you work with that? There's less and less room for work at this time. Journalists are being killed all over the world. They are trying to suppress all information.

HA: Look at Fukushima.

WA: Fukushima is the deadliest depression of all.

HA: I was reading about the invasion of Grenada in 1983 (after the Marines were killed in Lebanon), and the media response to the invasion of Grenada. I never realized there were actually no photographs. The island was cordoned off, and there was no press photograph of what occurred on the island.

WA: It was just a heinous invasion by a bunch of cowards, because they got blown up in Lebanon, where they basically ran away. And then they go and attack a defenseless Grenada. And try to make it a diversion, just to kill people as a diversion.

HA: As an example of a completely controlled media circumstance.

WA: We are full of all these unspoken crimes in all these circumstances that cost lives. I don't care about the money. Money comes and goes. I know that personally. I'm not blessed with any capital, and haven't been, and am working on things that haven't panned out yet. But to take lives is the bottom line. When you kill somebody, you can't replace that being, that person. This is what state security forces are constantly embodying. Like the circumstance in Egypt, for instance, completely outrageous. People say, "Oh Mubarak is out; Mubarak is out—the army didn't do anything," and I sense to myself that they will and they have. They have the martyr's wall up there to prove it. So we are talking about problems in Syria, problems in this and problems in that, while we have the energy crisis around the world. This whole idea that oil is always needed to run the empire, and we are looking for oil. This is one of the problems down in Venezuela right now, or in the Middle East. It sets up the oil flow to the West somehow. The Russian situation is a dangerous venture now.

HA: Nigeria and the Arabian Peninsula.

WA: Ah, Africa. I don't want to get started on that now, because Africa as a concept was created for the wealth of the capitalist system to operate. "Why don't the African American people want to work?" is that old Southern mentality. We did work for 246 years, for free. I'm not bringing that up as some kind of marker, but it is a marker and it has never been properly addressed.

HA: We were talking earlier about the inability to recognize when something is exhausted.

WA: Yeah. There seems no ability to do that. It is continuous digging and continuous digging and denial of the history of America. There is an interesting little book by Henry Steele Commager, an American historian, and it is not about this topic the way I am presenting it, but the title of the book is *Was America a Mistake?* And it is showing itself to ultimately be an experiment about a mistake. If the Keystone Pipeline goes through, for example, now. In other words, we're talking about the climate and we are talking about the survival of humanity. If the permafrost melts it's full of pathogens that can't be accounted for. We're not talking about something that is political here—I must emphasize this is not a political assessment. We are talking about life versus death. That is not too extreme to say, because of the general circumstance. It is not something you can talk about maybe in certain forums. In such forums they carry either a genteel or a hostile temperament, but these things are apparent now and are becoming more and more apparent with each day's news headlines. Even in a suppressed news environment, all these toxins are leaking out. Fukushima is the worst of all. It is potentially the total disaster. If it continues to go on, the former premier of Japan has talked about evacuating Tokyo. When we talk about evacuating a large city it is a chain reaction. So what's next? Beijing? The air pollution there is practically unbearable.

HA: You're talking about a totally different manner of life.

WA: Exactly.

HA: A Mad Max life.

WA: We were speaking about the lady who was enamored of freezing time at the plane of Mick Jagger and the Stones. You can't stop reality, because the Sun has been out there for over 4 billion years and is going to continue to burn and the Earth is going to continue to spin.

HA: And just because it goes through a period of time when it's not hospitable to human life, who cares right?

WA: Doesn't matter in the long run, because in 250 million years, even if it is still going to be hospitable, we will be blown away. And so it will be back to the way it was. We do not know what kinds of forms of life will pop up.

HA: It won't matter to us anyway.

WA: We are talking about things that are close at hand. We have our nerve endings, our feelings, so we have our concerns, and we do see another alternative that could be—that's why we are talking about this right now.

HA: That's right.

WA: So we do need to look in terms of creative language. I'm trying to work with different forms of expression, that's why I never settle on one genre.

HA: Right.

WA: Not just to do this and do that, but to have new kinds of ways of breathing. Putting all the pressure on one genre or one way of writing doesn't refresh it. Julio Cortázar always said that he never wanted to take advantage of himself, by just re-doing the same thing that he had mastered. Just take a chance on doing something different, or making friends with something that supposedly you shouldn't be making friends with—to cross borders, to re-engender yourself, you know, all the time. And that's what the poet is out here to do. He or she is a wanderer in the imagination, and you have to just take yourself into a position where you have faith in what you're doing. And too little faith is being exemplified. I mean, you have a large group of religious individuals in this world who have no faith in anything, nothing. If the car works, or if this comes on or if that comes on, that's fine. But if those things were taken away from me, I have no faith in anything.

HA: That's right.

WA: It's a test all the time, you know, to deal with an intentionally materialistic society without any materialistic capacity of one's own. We are going through that right now. It's not easy, and at the same time it opens you up to your work. I'm not saying we need to be opinionated to be creative people. I'm not saying that at all, but it does test your mettle, you know, to withstand contradiction and withstand need, and want and loss; I've dealt with a lot of that, and we all have.

HA: Yeah. But you're a testament to whatever drive, to whatever motivating force, because you seem to keep moving.

WA: Yeah. You want to keep moving. You don't want to stay in a sterile position. Sometimes you leave individuals that you don't want to leave, but because of motion you have to create this ongoing thing. So you don't destroy—but you keep moving. In other words, you're creating a time circle. Just like an orchestra: it needs a piccolo, it needs the bassoons, it needs the harp. It needs everything.

HA: It's a succession of movements.

WA: A succession of movements in order for all of that to make any kind of sense. To become sonorous you can't just have one particular instrument playing. You need all of these areas of coloration and nuance and sensitivity—and sometimes you need shrillness as well, and constant tonal movements.

HA: Dissonance.

WA: Dissonance! One of the great, great musicians died at 23. His name was Booker Little. He talked about dissonance making a sound bigger, and this is one of the things that has always concerned me. Because he passed away at 23, there's not enough written about him. And they have this idea in the Occident that you have to have put so many years in on this planet to deserve more comment. this gentleman had fused all the North African, Jewish and Middle Eastern sounds in jazz music at such an early age, which is just astonishing. And people don't know who he is. That's what we spoke about earlier, about adults who have zero knowledge base. And knowledge is something which, the more that you have awareness of it, continues to drive you forward, because you realize there are such gaps in what you know. I feel driven all the time because of all these gaps. Maybe a four-year-old in Mexico City knows more about something than I do now. So you never know. But you're not looking at it like that, not as competition. It's just awareness for yourself.

HA: Well yeah, I mean, there's different approaches to it. I mean, you're somebody who is very generous with your knowledge, and your knowledge and generosity with it is threaded into everything. It's not based on competition or one-upmanship.

WA: No, it's not about that. I wrote an aphorism about, you know, these conversations, where I know more than you and you know more than me, where we just want to compete with each other. That's something that's completely outside of what we need at this time. We need to have this collective movement of insight that allows healing of the brain, healing of the collective mind. This is something that Krishnamurthi pointed out. He says "insight heals." It cures these itinerant scars that are placed upon us by this insane repetition. For instance, "Jesus Christ is Lord and Savior," and you repeat over and over again this realia as if it sprang from a stunning isolation with no precedent in human reality. With the Egyptian chronicles eschewed from popular consciousness one is then stunted by a precarious view.

HA: In God we trust.

WA: In God we trust. Do we ask any questions about this?

HA: Is there any personal responsibility involved in that?

WA: None. We live by repetition; the repetition creates the truth of it. That's why the advertising industry so ingenuously made it out to the general mind in the 1920s, you know? Everybody knows about Bernays and mass-marketing. This was going on as early as 1923. This is not like a new situation, and it's stayed there since 1923—that basic model—all innovation in this society is based more on the details of something that's already been created. Nothing original. The computer is just an extension of the typewriter. In other words, all the prior technology is here as well, and so you're dealing with a cluttered environment. It is so cluttered with information.

HA: And those guys (Bernays, Lippmann), those early advertiser-propagandists, recognize that territory which you were talking about earlier, the area between dream and waking state, and then just totally co-opting it for advertising.

WA: That's amazing.

HA: I mean, it's incredible. It's incredible, thinking here is a new discovery, or here's a new territory that we've actually articulated in some way, or that we can actually explain to people to create a different context or understanding, and we're going to use it as a conduit for advertising.

WA: It's a conduit that creates capital. It's like the earlier circumstance we talked about: mass murder and genocide creates capital for the weapon's traders. For the advertisers the subconscious realms for them to explore and nutate via the setting in motion this desire and need for the product at hand. In other words buying extends the impalpable level. This is a compound-complex situation where no questioning transpires concerning existing behaviour in this sphere. And the whole idea of "Buy now and save"—how can you save if you're spending? But it's a trick. It's all based on tricks.

HA: If it doesn't work, then you're doing something wrong.

WA: In other words, it's like a poor person being blamed for not having money. So this is a completely worn-out scenario, but it's collectively approved to such a degree that anybody that says anything contrary to it tends to be isolated or labeled or painted with a certain kind of brush. But that kind of brush is irrelevant at this time, because we called it a *Titanic* situation. Who cares if you have a winning hand on the deck of the *Titanic*? I mean, will that accrue any kind of future? No. This is where we're at now. So, as I've said, we are in an isolated cosmos. It's amazing, it's out there and we have all this information, and the people on the ground are still blind, deaf and dumb. New galaxies, new cosmos, new this, new that, yet the history of the world is bottled up in a European cosmos—European facials, European motorcars. I mean, how did Europe get to be this way? You know, it's like the Guyanese thinker Walter Rodney who wrote the book, *How Europe Underdeveloped Africa*. I think his assassination was tied up with the publication of that book. So, this is far-out information. I mean, why follow yourself and commit suicide? This is the whole point. What are we talking about now? Is life a general suicide? You know, if you're on the side of life, that doesn't mean you're part of a political party or a part of this group or that group, because you have the instinct of life. You speak of life rather than death. All of our general rhetoric is based on demise rather than the propagation of life. It's always reduction rather than expansion.

HA: Right.

WA: And so life naturally expands. As you look at the cosmos it's always expanding. That's what a Stellar Nursery is about. You cannot control that. I mean, it's like we've been given a rhetoric that says that we can control the Sun and we can control everything that happens in the cosmos. It makes it feel as though we can control galaxies. But, this is a question I do ask everybody—used to ask everybody before I would do a reading: "Where is the Orion spur in the Milky Way?" And no one seems to respond. This is where our Sun is located on the Orion spur, where there exists other suns. This exists as our local star group.

HA: Where are we located?

WA: We are located near the edge of the Milky Way. It is specific stellar geography. It is this kind of insight that should be fostered in terms of education, in terms of where you're at, not what you're going to wear next month, etc. Where are you really at in the universe? And I think that the old Egyptian ideas are, for me, completely applicable because that's how I live, that right-brain understanding of the total rather than the partial. When you were becoming a scribe you understood by just writing things down, certain things about the self, and when the self starts to grow the other areas of interest begin to grow. This whole idea of the self contained in all areas of knowledge, whether it's geography or astronomy or jurisprudence—the understanding of the whole is always implicit in the part. But here, the parts are nothing but the parts. So I can't talk to a juridical student about work or personal theology because he or she is going to be locked in that little area. They can't cross-pollinate.

HA: That's right. Just their specialty.

WA: Yeah. I've been working recently with what I call infra-telepathy, where I'm dealing with my own telepathy like a circle. I'm putting something out and it flows around in a circle and comes back. I wrote a book recently, called *Infra-Telepathy*, but it was like in the doing of the book, I was hearing the phrases almost instantaneously. They were looping back to themselves—*boomboomboom*—so quickly I could barely write them down. It's that whole idea of farming the blood out and then re-injecting it into those areas for your own blood to heal yourself. They do it in German medicine and other places all over the world. I found that linguistically you can do it and you can re-engender yourself that way. You can be born out of a unicity and return to that unicity almost simultaneously. I was sparked by this book by this writer. I'm going to give you this book (Georgiana Peacher's *Mary Stuart's Ravishment Descending Time*). She's a friend of mine, she's a 94-year-old writer in Maine, and she wrote this amazing book about Mary Stuart, and the language in it is unbelievably brilliant, written in the 1970s. You can have it.

HA: Oh, thank you very much. It looks amazing.

WA: Yeah, she's an amazing writer. She is still active. I might call her today. She's 94 and she continues to create.

HA: This looks beautiful. It's amazing.

WA: I was touched by that book. I discovered her in England. I was over there and my friend Jonathan Skinner said, "Take a look at this." It sparked a language in me that I wrote all across the Atlantic Ocean. I wrote a book. She published this book in 1976.

HA: You've been traveling all over the place, right?

WA: I was moving around. I went through Miami to get the American Book Award, and then I went to England to do some talks at the University of London at Birkbeck.

HA: What was England like?

WA: Fantastic.

HA: Had you been there before?

WA: I hadn't been to England, in particular. The audiences were fantastic. They were rapt, very focused, very intelligent people. I gave a talk at Warwick in a reading with Alan Fisher, and a talk and reading at Birbeck, and then there was another reading I gave at another experimental locale in London.

HA: I saw you were there.

WA: Yeah? So, I've been in Seattle and Olympia, just came back from San Francisco. Did a reading at the Sacramento Poetry Center about a month ago. I'm going to Cornell like a week from today, a week from this coming Monday to read at Cornell and give some talks over there, and I'm going to read in Detroit in April. And then after that, I don't know. But, hopefully continue to move and—the real movement for me is to continue to work, continue to type, and type up older manuscripts that I've done and haven't gotten a chance to get to.

HA: That's hard to do.

WA: A lot of work, a lot of work. Because I work alone, I don't work with any help. And I'm an analog person—so I write it, I type it, and then I put it into the computer.

HA: I've worked with your typed manuscripts before.

WA: It's my hands-on idea. You know, I like to have written by feeling the electricity going through my hands, and when I type I actually edit it as I type it, and then once I put it on disk or something, it's done. It allows you to work quickly that way. It seems like it's slow but it works quickly for me, so I'm not going through a bunch of drafts and stuff like that. So I'm running out of here and I'm going to go out and do some work today and see what I come up with on this play and continue to go forward. See how the publishing projects transpire, you know, with different presses. I'm waiting on certain books and certain things to come through. You never know if it's this or that or that or this. Nevertheless, in the long run you're working through on the bigger picture, on the whole project. I'm working on this huge alchemical project, the alchemical nature of language and how that language can transmute the human condition. It seems grandiose, but it does work, point by point by point, until it blooms in a certain way. And I'm also concerned with the environment, the nature of the environment. It seems to be pushing in this direction, unfortunately, because of the pollution we spoke of with post-Fukushima, the social deterioration. What is the cosmos, in other words? What is this thing that we are in? That's never asked. Why is there something rather than nothing? That's what I would like to know. No one asks that question. Instead they say, "You were born in this year, that year, you were born in this city or that city," which you have no control over. So that becomes an issue in American popular culture, about age grouping and class grouping, where you came up: "Oh, I came up there" "Oh, I came up there, too"—and that's supposed to create some kind of relationship. That's not true affinity.

HA: For all we know, we could all be on the verge of the next Permian extinction.

WA: Yes, the Permian extinction. We don't fully know the extent to the powers that have been put in motion.

HA: We can have affinity from that—we can all be in the same fossil layer.

WA: The complexity of the human experience reduced to a fossil layer. This is a criminal situation. You do need to have a consciousness, to get to that expansive understanding.

HA: Yeah.

WA: That's what education should be about, but it's not. Not just giving facts to remain, but to expand. The school systems are tragically poor. I'm primarily talking about Harvard, Princeton, Yale.

HA: Well, that's incredible. My two kids—the youngest one just got out of elementary school, and I was amazed. I grew up in California, went to a public school. They went to public school in California, and the curriculum: I would say 95% of it is exactly the same.

WA: Really?

HA: Yeah, I'm serious. It's crazy. And my version of the 95% that we share is circa the mid-50s. It was already archaic in my day. Literally, the same thing, the same years, the same units at the same time.

WA: It's not applicable to the situation.

HA: Yeah. I think their schools are considered to be good schools, because they actually can execute the ancient curriculum at all. Do you know what I mean?

WA: For children, I'm of the opinion that, you know, the method in (not the Montessori is it? the Steiner school!)—that children shouldn't have to read and do anything until they're about eight, and just do visual work, kind of come into it on their own. To tell you the truth, I didn't really learn from just reading until I was eight-and-a-half.

HA: It worked for you.

WA: It worked for me. But how many kids get through in this kind of system?

HA: Yeah. It's true.

WA: I almost slipped through the cracks. But thanks to a great teacher, and my mom who was on me about this, I got through it. But you know, this is something, that the school system is completely inadequate. And certain so-called conservative people will say the same thing—that the system is completely non-workable. Like the little ones we saw, you know, two- and three- year-olds, I mean that's when you start to get them, start to work with them. A consciousness, not forced to stay inert until subsumed by the drug culture.

HA: Well just the whole idea that the math system is based on the decimal.

WA: Mhm.

HA: That's all they learn. They don't learn binary. They don't learn anything. They don't learn any of the other kinds of systems that are prevalent and potentially useful.

WA: These are the prevalent ones.

HA: They don't, and that's just insane.

WA: Backwards. In other words, it's completely backwards. How are you equipped to live if you have no means of living, and no tools to live? It's impossible. It's a real problem. You're just a five-year-old, an eight-year-old, and you're given this bad education. I got a bad education, I must admit it. A really bad education.

HA: Me too.

WA: We didn't get a chance to do languages. We had a chance to do nothing. I was a gym rat. I ended up as a gym rat for a long time until I got to the point where I got sick of hanging out in gyms and talking about the NBA. I found something else.

HA: That's right. You were a Los Angeles Unified student, yes?

WA: I was.

HA: So was I.

WA: L.A. Unified is typical, man. Down there where I was at, nobody hardly made it out of there. Only a few of the cats made it out of there. It's an isolated situation. You've got to keep going on your own without the so-called encouragement that you get in so-called upper-class schooling systems. I meet you, I meet other people, it works, but individuals have to do a lot of their work by themselves—be that lone fragment that magnetizes other lone fragments in order to commence alchemical communication.

HA: Well, and the only thing: to whatever extent I am saved or was saved from that was however I was exposed to music and books.

WA: Exactly. Following a certain lead or something like that. I mean, I discovered John Coltrane and all that when I was 13, so I didn't go to the parties and get swallowed up in lifelong distraction. I didn't get spun around by one of the gorgeous girls, ending up a slave of the child support system. That's the dealio man, to just get by, by the skin of your teeth. Everything is fighting against you all the time. Everything wants you out of the way. But you have to continue and handle yourself in a way that allows a certain kind of...there's no answers for it. There's no way you can make up an answer about how we got here to this point where we can have this conversation—no way. It's just magical, man. It's like grace. Grace is part of it.

HA: Just like we were saying earlier: there has to be some capacity to be able to hear it. You hear it or you are steered by it, or however you want to characterize it.

WA: You have to have a hearing of it somehow. It's the luck of the draw. Everybody wants a cookie-cutter idea. It's like doing writing classes and having students.

HA: Mhm.

WA: They're kind of looking for answers: "How do you do this. How do you do that?" You can't give them answers. One thing about writing—you can't get answers about writing. It has to be done in the doing. I just let everyone know that I don't have any objective standards about how they're going to go about doing something. But you do have to find yourself, and I ask everybody to weigh their hands: their offhand and their central hand. And they say, "Oh, they weigh different. They feel different. One feels lighter than the other." I say, "Yeah." And you were born at a certain time and a certain place. And I'm not using some kind of strict astrology, but I'm saying that you have a certain temperament. Everybody does have a certain temperament and needs to be able to follow their own leading according to that temperament.

HA: That's right.

WA: That way they can begin to sculpt it into something real, for themselves, you know? And, that means something to them, in that way. The reading will not just become an assignment. It will be an organic experience, which is never a bad thing. It doesn't mean you're going to know everything, that you will be a complete expert on this or that, but that's not what the writer is about.

HA: Right. And the knowledge in that sense that we were talking about before—it's not a competition thing. It's not about entering into a secret society by virtue of what you know. It's about that kind of appropriateness for your time and place, and what it is to actualize yourself.

WA: That's exactly right.

HA: That's a difficult lesson, you know.

WA: That's a difficult lesson, because everything is valued otherwise.

HA: Valued otherwise.

WA: Valued otherwise. The value system is askew at this time, at this level. It's completely askew.

And Then, In Here

Harold Abramowitz

It was one, or it was the other. That much, and violence. If you were a prince. That was the way the picture wanted to go. To put up its fists and fight. But we were broken for the way we spoke of mediation. As if your emotions were better than anyone else's. It was in the way we looked at time. It told us all sorts of things. I was walking. I was eating food from the palm of my hand. And then I wondered what the point was.

Troubling times. It is the force that folds the violence, that calls us names. I am a junior lying in my casket. And that was before you believed in me. What I would then say to you is about the state of my heart. I was a child, a junior. But we call each other by name all the time. And the way we are falling now is even more meaningful than it was, at first. But who knows. It takes all kinds. And then bright colors. And then you are feeding me feeling.

And then you want to tell me that the world is this way or that way. I was walking on my knees. I put my hands in my pockets. And then you asked me something. I ran out of the house, crying. I put my hands in my pockets and told you that I was going to feel much better.

*

This becomes the summer much better than anything else. That was an old pattern. But then you call it behavior. A violent struggle. It was beyond belief. I would say it was. It was in the way you looked at me. I was in the hall, and I had my hands out. I was turning red. It was all the time. There was no way we could find our way around the room. I put a better face on this by asking what the red in the room was all about. So, you wanted to say to me. There were various faces. It was funny to put it all together. That much. I was telling you. There were more things in the house that we had to make decisions about. I was walking in the hall. I wanted to run, but I kept thinking the same old things. I was in the bedroom, first. I was putting my best foot forward.

And, even then, I might have felt better about myself had I been able to see things more clearly. And then I was finding out a little bit more. It was hurting me. I could see myself turning around, or rather, away. There was the prettiest angel on the ceiling. This was exactly like the way it was supposed to be, I thought. I kept asking for things, but you couldn't hear me. I thought a lot about you. And then I was turning around. There was a footstool in the doorway. I couldn't believe that you were who you said you were. I wanted to have something to eat. It was a warm day. I thought I believed in you. It was in the morning. I was wanting a lot of things, at that point. I was in the hall, and I thought that I would say something to you. I would move forward. I would put my best foot forward. But that was because of the way I was looking forward to things. I couldn't believe that there was something in there.

*

You were waiting there. I had to put my head down. It was not funny because the time was beginning to move by very quickly. Then, suddenly. I fell apart. It was up to me. I looked up and down the hall. I felt like I could accurately assess the whole situation just by looking around. I started to move very slowly. I wanted to find out how much things would cost. It was sort of incredible to think, I thought, that this thing could so readily replace that thing. There was a mirror in the hall. I think my face was burning. And what do you think the chances are of hearing some good news today? I asked. I was waiting for my dreams to come true. But then it was violent. It was how I felt. The way emotions move from one thing to the next. In time for dinner. You could see me from where you were sitting on the couch. I was wondering about the ways of the world, or rather, origins. How the world was born. I am old, I thought. I am thinking a million things at one time. And the river runs in the house and there are all kinds of things that run after me and torture me, I thought. All because of the way I become when I think of you,

I said. Your heart is all aflame. You put your glasses on and wait for me by the furnace, the fire. I was warm enough as it was. I couldn't wait because I was angry and hungry at the same time, I thought. And then I was looking for a fight.

*

I am tired, I said, of being vague. There was a kernel of truth in what I said. I was in the house. I put my things up for sale. My things were rare and valuable, and I used to love and take care of my things, too, I said. I heard you say that you were angry, that I had warmed up too quickly for your tastes, as it were. I protested that I had never been comfortable in that place. That I had continually put myself in the worst positions. Because of the way you looked at me. I forgot what I was going to say. I wanted to tell you that you were exactly what you thought you were, but I am in the house, and then I am in the hall and none of it matches or makes any kind of sense. It is a little bit like a fraud, or a swindle, or even a puzzle, I think. The way you talk. I could see you from where I was sitting on the couch.

*

I confess that I feel things, but then there is an authorization process that takes place. A way to make me believe that I am on the right track. I say, for instance, that you are Romeo and Juliet. I pick my things up off the kitchen floor. It is a perfect day. There is a box of potentially good and usable things that I have left on the back porch, I think. I can't believe my face looks just the way I say it does. But, then, I barely know you. If I could picture you, I think, I would know you better. But then you ask for something. I am sitting in my room. I see that the walls are painted a very pleasing color. I can't believe it, though, when I am looking at you. If only I were to become someone else, I think. I think I am very happy. I can see you from where I am sitting at the kitchen table. The day is young, and there is really nothing else that I need to be doing, at that point. I really wish that I could see your face every morning when I wake up, I think. Each and every day there is some kind of scene. We make a scene between us. I can see you from where I am standing in the hall. You can't just submerge your face in the water so suddenly, I think. You can't just make things up, make them happen that way, I think.

*

So, when you are standing there, and it feels very emotional to say that we are in here, that we are in this house together, again. I was walking down the hall. And it would be just as violent anywhere else, I thought. Anywhere else in the house that I would care to go, I thought. Whatever the excuse might be. I don't know why I would even want to resist, I thought. I could tell you the things I know. I was waiting for you to call me. I thought. I wanted you to pay attention to me, but we were both very distracted, at that point. I can feel. I thought. It was not nice, and I was not a very nice person. But I wanted to be able to say that there was something in the world for me. I could have said the same thing. What you were feeling. That I should have stayed inside that day. But on the outside it is funny that we sometimes feel like we are free, I think. I look up and say it. Who is trying to scare you? I ask. I want to sit in the living room all day long. There is nothing else that I am doing or feeling, at that point. And this, in spite of what we are thinking and talking about at any given time.

*

You might have asked me what I was waiting for. It was a quiet day. I was standing on the street. There was a lot to do. And the houses in this part of town are extremely well-constructed, I thought. "Why, with a little bit more money." I started to say to you. You are standing on the same part of the front porch as I am. In the same part of the house. And it was as if you were going to turn me around. Hey, I could see you from where I was standing on the front porch, I said. I can feel. I could see you from where I was standing on the porch. I painted the front of the house a nice shade of green for just that reason, I thought. The question remained kind of hanging in the air, though. So this was in a house, and the house was many stories high. Something I was wondering. How life was easy. How nothing is easy at first. It was funny to say that the thing was true, that life was easy, that nothing is easy at first, whether it was true or not. In any case, the day was making me feel like a failure. I put on my favorite song. And then I realized. Suddenly. That I was put here for a reason, too.

And no matter what I want to ask you about, I say. I say that I am feeling a little bit stung by your indifference to my style of house decorating. To my aesthetic, in general. At first, of course, there was nothing wrong with the way you saw me. As violence. What I was going to do or say, in the first place. What I was going to say, in the first place, was that I was glad to be there. In that place. There could have been so much more, though. Or that's what I thought. What I was thinking, at that point. I was thinking for a purpose, a reason. And whatever you said to me, at that point, was true. It was going to be quite alright in the end, I knew. However, I was starting to look and act like a real phony. There was something really phony about the way I felt, what I was thinking, at that point. I think I just sat in the sun and stared for a really long time. And then I found myself standing in the hall. It was like a dream. I set all of the things that I had in my pockets in a row on the table in the hall. And if I get to live anywhere else, I thought, it would be in a house on a cliff, overlooking an ocean. I think that I would like to live in a house with a view of the ocean, I thought. And then I am seeing you very clearly for the first time in a long time. There was something new in the room. Something new in the house. The way we are living, I think. I could see you from where I was standing in the front yard. I was shaking with excitement for what I felt, for what I knew to be true. How I could cover my own tracks, if I wanted to. And I was already stepping very lightly, very delicately, I thought. And in that very special way that only I knew. In fact, I could tell you. I could reach out and touch you, too, I thought. Inasmuch, as that was also true. It was what I said it would be. I had to look all over the house just to find my hat, my keys, my coat. It was very beautiful in the house, at that time. Just like you might have observed, I thought. Here are all the mementos, things, I thought. I asked myself whether I wanted something to eat. I could have said that that was also true for you, at that time. Also true for you. I could see you from where I was standing in the hall. I put my hands out. I was looking for a fight. I don't really fight all that often, I said.

*

And I was asking you questions. It was a funny thing to say, at that point. Then I looked at the door. It was summer. I was in the house. I thought I could hear you moving. It was funny to walk around on the carpet. I could see you from where I was sitting on the front porch. But I think I was in a panic. There was something there. Or some reason or another that I had to imagine. I was facing panic. Still, I always had something to say. I think the emotion of the moment was getting to me. I thought, perhaps, about too many bad things. Why, I asked myself, would I think about so many bad things. I remembered bad things. I imagined bad things. And then I asked myself whether or not I was even a good person. I put my hands out. And then I remembered to ask you. It was in the house and there were a lot of good things to look forward to. I wasn't afraid of the weather. I put my hands out. I tried to remember what I was supposed to be doing. I polished all the brass around the living room. It was morning. I felt good. I didn't think it would be wise to do anything too differently, not at that point. And then I asked you what you wanted. I was putting my best foot forward. I would think, I said. I would provide for you, I said. I took a deep breath. There is a reason that I find the things I am looking for so quickly, I thought. I needed a nap. I put my hands out. I put my best foot forward.

*

It was in the morning, and I was in the kitchen. You live on a shelf, I laughed. And all afternoon I could see you. I was filled with vision. There was definitely something there. In the morning. I was trying out any number of different things, at that point. I was putting my best foot forward. And then I saw you. I thought that I would turn to you. I remembered that I was in the house. I could not remember anything better than that, anything more than what I was thinking, at that point, I thought. I could hear you. I could even see you. But, then, I would have to have turned my head. I live very much lower, I thought. Or, perhaps, I live near. Or perhaps none of it matters. Or all of it, except the turning around, that is. And then what I suspect to be the truth. And the truth, as it turns out, is very different than what I thought it was.

Maybe I liken you to an angel. I might be seeing you sitting over there. The folds in your hands. Sometimes I like to stress that it is you, an angel, that I am thinking of. I like to think that I remember your garment. The specific folds in your garment. I put my best foot forward each time I try to take a walk, I think. And then things get slower. They slow down. There is the ribbon. There is a kind of book. And then there is isolation. You are my benefactor. And then I say that the truth is strange, large, or that it is strange. It takes me a lot longer to beg, I think. I have my pride, you know.

*

I am in the house. I like to say. I am on my knees. But if I put my best foot forward, I will think of a million things to do, and, even, all at once. I will step this way and that way, I think. That there is so much to do. That I can even say there is trouble. That I like to smell trouble. Or this is what I say. Your. Money. Comes at me. I value a car over a dish. I am perverse for thinking so, I think. I am on the ground, I think. This is my neck, my shoulders. What I told you was the very first thing on my mind. It is ringing in my neck. And every time I turn around I see that you can see me, too.

*

It was a specific day at home. There was a bright sky. I folded my hands and legs. I might have told you something. Something I lied about. It does depend on the way you sit, and where you put your feet, I think. How you cross your legs. If I were at home. If I wanted to say something to you. It was going to rain. And then your intention. Like a little bit bad. You just don't know where anyone comes from, I said. I lived in the house, and then I put my hands in my pockets. I decided that I was going to take a walk. It was an unparalleled level of intensity. I felt. The best and the worst of things, all at one time. I feel that my fingers are too small, I say. I tell you that it was just a dream, that there was no telling. I don't think I believe in what I can see, at this point.

Then parts of the house call to me. I have to go and not scream quite as much as I am used to doing. I want to fight the feeling. I can feel. If I have to put my best foot forward all the time. I say that I am fighting. I am committed to fighting. And things being as such. If I was going to go and see you one day, even though I was fighting a feeling of panic. I put my thoughts towards good things. I could feel the feeling come and want to get me. I put my best foot forward and started running because I was so scared. And that's not all. I looked bad. I felt bad. I was in my current situation solely because of the way I was feeling, I thought.

And if need be, I would drop. It was impossible to see the sun. The day was very cloudy. There were very many tears. And there was heat. And there was a move that I was going to make. I thought that I was in motion. I put my best foot forward. I thought you could see me from where you were sitting on the couch. I was like a star. It was in the middle of all of this thinking that I asked you if you wanted to get married. It didn't matter what you said. I could hear what you were thinking. And to think that I was in the middle of it all. I put my hands out. I felt my face hot in the sun. Yesterday seems like such a long time ago, I thought. And it's funny in here. Your language as a result of my feeling. I was on time. I met the moment head-on. There was no tomorrow. But to make that much, or to mean that much. In the end, I was going to come around. I was going to see myself through. It is like you say. You belong home. I was not going to find myself in difficult positions anymore. I took a vow. I had to believe that it could possibly be true. But I don't have a concept of such things anymore, I said.

*

No, not really, I said.

*

And you were going to say that I only got married because of how bad things looked. So I looked up at the sky, and there was a lot to say and do. The house, even. It was like a dream, even. There was something breaking, and the places that I felt I could go, if I had to go. I could see you from where I was sitting on the couch. It was a clear and sunny day. The night was clear. I could see the moon from where I was standing in the backyard. But how could I, I thought. I let myself slip very badly, I said. It was like poison, or it was like a door that was opening and closing and causing us all kinds of trouble or disease. So I was looking at where I might have been. I think slowly. I think dead. I think all the same things, all the time. And this because the kitchen is what it is and I don't have anything to ask you about. Not then, especially not when I was putting my best foot forward.

*

And it is not idiotic in the least, I said.

*

But it was incredible to think. To be looking up so quickly. Like I was used to the way things were. I sat in the kitchen. I was in the house. A house, if you will. And then I was asking about some of the things you were familiar with. You wanted to say that to me. I could explain that tomorrow was okay, too. Peace of mind. A hidden spot. This is what you tell me. And if the birds don't make me run. And if I am sitting here and wondering what the next move is going to be. And if I couldn't tell a lie, not then, not at that point. But I do want to tell you that there is a spot in the backyard, and we could get to that place. I think I have to believe in all the things I smell and eat and touch and taste. Even all the things in the kitchen, at that point. There is much to live for, I thought. I would think the scent from the kitchen is strong. What is cooking right now? I ask. This is what I tell you. If there is a reason for it. For what I might say to you. But the challenge is to move successfully from one part of the house to the next. I am not the boss of my situation at all. Not if I want to be. But then there is summer to think about as well.

*

It was one wish after another. And it really was wishing because that's what I said it was. The day of judgment was upon us. Or rather, I mean that what I say is modern. It's because I live so well that things backfire. There was a certain amount of smoke that came out of the house, at that point, but it wasn't really anybody's fault. It was morning. I had to stop worrying about my hair. I was going to look the way I was going to look, no matter what. Fundamentally, I was what I said I was going to be. There was a much better way of asking how things could have become so damaged, though. And then what we say to each other. What you were saying. I was putting my head, or rather, my ear against the wall. And this was because of how hard it had rained the night before. I swear I was right about everything. I was looking for you. The color of the sky. The way it looked. I was very sure about you. It then occurred to me that I was not the best person for the job. I put my best foot forward. I beat my fist against the wall. How do I say this to you? I could put it in the form of a letter. I am always thinking about the way I might correspond with you. I put my head, or rather, my ear against the wall. This was because of the way I felt about things at that time. It was a little bit like sleeping on the couch, or sleeping on the floor. There were so many things going on. I could tell by the way you looked at me. I could see the house from where I was standing on the street. You could not have said it to me any more clearly. This is what I wanted to hear, though, but could not tell you about. The occasion was, perhaps, wrong. Each one of us has to look better each and every day, I thought. We have to start looking much better, I thought. It was the way I looked at you. I could hear the water dripping from the kitchen sink. I thought it was a little bit funny. It was funny to be thinking something so intimate about myself, at that point. I could hear the water dripping from the kitchen sink. I don't think there was a leak. I have no good ideas, I said. I said this to myself. Would there be a better occasion for this kind of communication? I wondered. At some point I would tell myself the reason. I would answer my own questions about what was going on, but then, I think I needed to remember something. There was something I couldn't remember. I could see you in my mind's eye. I thought it was funny to say so. But there was nothing good that was going to come of any of it. I thought about the work I was doing and why there were always so many alternative ways, methods, of getting things done. I might have been holding you back. It was productive to think about, I thought. I could see you from where I was standing in the hall. I was never invited over again. I liked the way the air smelled. I put my fingers out the window. I wanted to feel the wind against my fingertips. It was a very emotional day for me. Too many things, I thought, had fallen by the wayside. I was sitting in the kitchen. And over by the counter. I thought that I might have a little more to say about the way things were going, what was going to happen next, but I needed inspiration. And then I started to think about all the things that I might have said to you. I put you in the first position. It was not going to hurt me. I meant to say that it was not going to hurt me as bad as I thought it might have, but that was the way I was framing my thoughts, at that point. I thought a little bit about what I might say to you. It was almost the end of the season by then. At that point, I was falling asleep. I thought it was rude. It was almost morning. You could have heard a pin drop. I was in the house. I was not planning to continue. Not that there weren't many good reasons to continue, I thought. You could see me from where you were sitting on the couch. We were smiling in the picture. From that point on, I think I lived out of time. From that moment on, I lived out of time. The focus of my thoughts had certainly shifted. There was very little left to say. I don't think I had any other way out of what I was thinking. I sat in the kitchen. I looked at my face in the light. I could easily have been dreaming. But there were things that I wanted to say. I was something of an expert, a dreamer, an expert. Or that is what you say. How do you find yourself saying what you believe, I wondered? It was an extremely maddening moment. A time. There was something about the way things were put that caused a great deal of trouble. I was filled with a kind of wanderlust, or distress. You supported me directly by the things you said to me. I should have smiled more. Inside of two hours, all of it would have been over, I thought. I put on my hat and gloves. I moved to the backyard. I could no longer see the light. I had it all planned. I could see you from where I was standing in the yard. You were there. You were in the house. There was a position that I would take up, but only in a certain light. A certain way that I would stand. I had to stop myself from singing, from even thinking about songs or music. What I might say to you at any given time. There was something that was very easy for me to say about the way things were constituted, at that point. I loosened my collar, a little. There were birds flying overhead for most of the morning. You could see me from where you were standing in the backyard. I was trying to stand straight and tall. You had picked a perfect number. There was nothing else I could do. There were many pictures of us on the walls. It was like walking into a house again. A home. I had no opinion about things. The way things were constituted was of no concern to me. I would tell the story of our home, of how strange I sometimes felt in the place I lived. I liked the way I would face the music. I thought. It was better than talking to you. I could see the sky. I loved the way things looked at noontime. And the backyard. It was all so beautiful. We walked together. The way you looked at me. You could see me from where you stood in the hall. A terrific noise was taking place. You could almost see the front porch in a very clear way from where we were standing on the street, I thought. I wondered if you were sick. I wondered whether I'd somehow stepped over the line in a rotten way.

*

I could see that. If you could see that. Touching it. A version. Really touching it. Likewise, you said to me. But I am struggling. I am certain you can see that. As soon as I call your name. Taking sides. It is beautiful in here. I was at home all day. I could see what you were up to. And there was an envelope in the mailbox. Everyday we look at each other in the same way. There is a way to look at this more kindly, more broadly, I thought. I am moving my neck in and out of harm's way, I thought. And then every second. It was a really, really nice day.

*

I don't think I have to have a perfect fit, I said. So, that was a way of saying what I was going to say in the first place. It all feels so good and clean and wholesome. I was wondering about how fast things would happen. I was sitting in the house, and you were telling me something. You think you have dreams. It was in the room. There was some version of this place. I asked a lot of foolish questions, at that point. I was in the house, and I was hoping that I would see you. I was in the kitchen. I was waiting for the perfect moment to say something to you. I saw that things were changing. There certainly were a lot of difficulties. I could see you through the window in the living room. What a wonderful thing for you to have asked me about. And then I asked myself. I sit by the window in the living room. I think I feel that I am growing in very positive directions. It is like I am sitting on the couch all over again. There are so many things in the hall, at that point. I could see you from where I was standing in the hall. And the windows are always facing me. I am always facing forward. What I once said. I see the television in the living room. I can see the antenna on the roof from where I am standing in the backyard. I am putting two and two together because it is today and because today holds together very nicely. So, when I was going. Coming to the house, early, and very often. I had to put two and two together in order to survive. I had to say hello to you just as soon as I entered the house. I was sitting in the kitchen. It was an old story. You tell me something. I say something, too. I have nothing left to live for, or that's what I want to tell you. So we are sitting in the garden. This happens every year at springtime. I am always looking over my shoulder. I am feeling a great deal of affection for things. There are a lot of stories that I want to tell you. We said that we would meet. I put my hand out. The weather is bound to get worse, I think. Just as hot as can be, my hands, but I don't care. I shouldn't be the one complaining, the one who has to answer you. I want. I love. I need evidence. Each morning you came into the room and watched what I was doing. I put my hands out. I think I am going to go for a walk. It's a surprise. You might have said something else to me. If I'd said something else to you, what do you think, imagine, it would have been, at that point I can see you from where I am sitting on the couch. There is music playing. I am in the house. It is warm in here because it is a very warm day. There is something I want to tell you about. And then you walk into the room. You are walking into the room. It takes some time to say that I am in the middle of the room. I am feeling very good about myself. I can only ask the question. I am feeling much better by this time because of all the work that's been done around the house. But then the despair sets in. It has something to do with the time, that time in particular. A revolution, even. It supports me when I have to say that the end is not the end, but is, rather, a beginning. You could see me from where you were sitting in the living room. I think I felt brave, at that point. I was going to say something to you. Or, rather, there was something that I wanted to say to you. I have to have a nice appearance. I could hear the music from the speakers in the living room. We were in the house. At that point. I was going to say that the house was really very large. We were in the house. I could hear water dripping from the kitchen sink. And you are just incredible, I thought. I wanted to say that we were sitting in the backyard and that we were sitting in the house and that, just then, there was something on the lawn, that there was an explosion. Maybe in the garden. But when you say that. Sitting in the kitchen is a very special kind of decision to make, I think. I was starting to think things backwards, to do my housework in reverse. I love the photograph, I said. And then in the bedroom. You were standing in the backyard, talking on the telephone. It was a significant moment, an event, in our personal history. I could see you from where I was standing in the kitchen. I would liked to have made a quick decision. I was hoping that the perfect plan would come to mind when I needed it to. Would I even recognize the perfect plan if it came to me, came to mind? I wondered? And then I yawned, stretched. I put my best foot forward. I'd never even thought about the weather, not at that point. And each time I turned around. It was almost like you were at the point of breaking, or, rather, you were taking things into account. I wondered aloud for a second time, at that point. What you thought about the work that had been done in the kitchen. How things might have been changing. I can't wait for you to see the hall, I said. I thought it was funny to say so, too.

POEMS: INDELIBLE ROTATIONS
Will Alexander

Pre-Cognitive Volation
Will Alexander

The Iridescent Enigma

"In this smokeless harrier desolation
I have surmounted inscrutable errata
      under two electric polar moons
shifting between the colours of slate-blue & magenta

I the Andean Hill Star
hovering in these Martian x-ray wastes
the iridescent enigma
my centripetal wings
beating against the soul of cartographical surcease
with its enervated distension
with its migrating sun loss

the triple atmosphere corroded
by tense elliptical static
by the drainage from barbarous glacial nerves
so that the strange contentions of Phobos
      make the human staggering genetic
less & less a factor
where ciphers are beheaded

humankind
now tending to gaze from a portico of gangrene
from model as nervous collective

so I am alone
having absorbed isolation
having absorbed the general colouration of imbalance
isolated by planet
from *Augastes lumachellus*
from *Lophornis magnifica*
in an alien enigma
alone

I have left the Earth & its species
incapable of self-rescue
of the dazzling vapour which transmutes
which allows the watery chemicals to rise
& take on the wisdom of vertical misnomer
of the acid which would blend
with the aerial oxide waters
with the prepotent force of natural helium speech

which implodes
which transcends present character
constricted as it is by anorexia & debris

its retention corrosively split
into an oblong grain which ceases
like a bleak 'Siberian witch' in tragic forms of respiration

its sodium
kindled by fractions which torment
which hounds the aspiration
as to apogee
as to consuming volation

so I as hummingbird
as expanded broach points in the blood seeking elongation
      & task
which conflagrates interia

again
the task
so that illuminates snake through the cells
no longer palpable as visual largesse
as silken sanguinary spectrums
to be bled
& negatively fed to half-learned upheavals

I
who now live
above the liminal burst
which exists
between that which flies
& that which stays sullied

no
I am not marooned on opthalmic plateaus
        cartographically contained
as though Peru were the only distance
        the only mercurial diamond to be breathed
to be absorbed as exclusive monomial clarity
so the barrenness
the solemn gamma-ray gradations
the probing snows on Olympus Mons
with its scattered rays
with its geometric diamonds
congealed in the orbit of blackened sphinxian diameter

which gives me claim
to magical fluxation & mist
so that my 5 former bodies example gives to my aura
a fabled discipline & a marker
& a glance which traces odour
according to hieroglyphic substance capable of plentitudes
        & aggressions capable of neurological dis-affirmatives

here I am
woven by gravitational nobility
yet of free & cold space
known throughout the yellowed Saturnian inveiglements
or across the Uranian methane formations
or in the Oort configuration
where a basic elevation is opened
where pre-turpentine milling
of the living & the living dead
are both broadened & destroyed

so that the atmosphere
an earthly debility of garrisons
becomes
a cancelled habitat for being

yes
for dense & offensive procurement
so that
the holocaust of tribes
the central extermination of salt
is no longer that which will flower
in a post-racial Kemet
being
the aboriginal darkness which pre-exists time

again
the invisible fever
which opens in the being
a random helium morale
a pitch of nigredo
of a cinder inside a cinder
which post exists the inverse
called by gross existence
a pre-directional Eden

so one can never explain
the pure charisma of my zodiac
the instant bell of my zodiac
under the Christian law of simple post-mortem carnage

never a blame cast by twists & thickets de-invaded
& then annulled
by natural solar crystallization
known to varied shifts
& different anatomies of creation

here I am
graspless
a Kemetic eclipse incantation
which overcomes the vile
by he
who migrates from nectar
who unmingles barley
by he who detracts weight"

The Blood Penguin

"I am the carnivore
the hounded night walker
searching for my scattered under glass

they claim I should return to monomial transfixing
to exhibit A & no further

to some
I am six foot & lizard

to others
I am considered a mange lamb
returned from the tropics

I am never given due as to sum or proportion
I am seen as the source of something leprous
as no longer the motive of who I was thought I was shaped to be

I who live as mislaid damage
as part of pointless verbal ejecta

there are no nouns to ensnare me
to fish up blood so as to summon consensus

I am never that condition within the fire of conjoinment

I am never to be
the human boy genius
the archivist
the bartered child contending with study

I am none of the above
none of the aforesaid compendiums

I am the animist
the vertical lion tundra
the diamond bird who burrows under snow

because of my leaning
I know the stark Egyptian soma
much as would a blinded cemetary scribe

& because I understand
one's basic neural unravelment
I am seen as piacular
as spectre
as both standing & freezing
being of some other form
from some other planet

as clinical moray addendum
this contains in itself
blackened scrawl marks from Moravia from squandered quanta
    from the Sunda Islands
from quaking fogs from Santiago

they say I suffer from powerful deafening by resistance
my eyes wild & in-ferocious with lapses

the attention span blunted
the astrological paralysis shifted

so they say the unknown is the trigonomic
is the transcended nucleus
the born equational spell
according to the flaws in universal summoning

I am ancient pantomime who cannot grasp
who cannot transgress his inherited Landino

as to Mayan glyphs & squares
I am plummeted
I am simply without the means to conduct my own prism

to take on the culpable mean
at circumstantial limit

I exist through negated practical limit through parallel sub-causes
without knowing the desire
to seek the enzymes of living

I am without & without & without

I who create doubt & the genetics of perpetual conflict

I could be strange as a human half wrought
who poses himself as Ilario Pozuelos

& what is claimed against me
is not unreasoned
is not the treatise of post-fanatics

instead
it is a curious treatise on circumstantial exhibit

it says
my values are possessed by distance
like someone humbled or plagued by a treaty

my dispossessed senses
described by these methods
under the forms of the treasonous

it tells me I am lifeless blood equipment that my genes
            are not useful
that my mind is simply stricken or exposed

yet such a chronicle loses spores in the glaciers
it says
I am of Africa & the sea coast
of Ghana & the Seychelles
of insular breakage near the Azores

yet it states my non-placement
my cavern
my debilitating refuge

not even a dwelling beneath the stars
as etheric camp base on Saturn

such is the ether climb
the sub-revelation as dialectical cartography
conjoining with the ocelots
swimming across the prisms of Mauritius

or simple flatland in Manchuria

these are seen as soils no known warrior can claim

because I readily announce my resistance
my tone as carnivorous scarring wandering beyond pervasive
            death concussives

claimed
by genetic dis-logistics
by anarchic ruin
by Jurassic sibling serosas

I cannot describe by cursory enclosure external motivation
or any rotary or back-flowing water attainment

it is described as simulacra
as ghost data
as hibernation through pillage
non-specific
post-necrotic
partaking in part as jonquil & longevity

of course the cells blaze
infinity evolves
the monsoons project through containment

yet nothing resolves
nothing forbears & is clement

I exist
as steep electrical ice
asking of myself spells
of pointless dominating fuels

within this agnostic current
I describe
myself as one who's hellish
who's buried his weight with double insistence
who seems to sleep in a brazen cylinder of peril

then after a pause in listening
calling myself The Blood Penguin embraced by squalls
by an oily & misshapen blinding"

from Concerning the Henbane Bird

"...this is why I've returned from the dead
        as the great poltergeist who wanders
who darts through salted manganese ruins
        giving document to the inclement

this is why I land on spotted neutron logs
        on defective bullocks & grass
to test the arcane leaning of the world
its projection
its exhibit beyond disrupted stomas

so through spillage
through countless myrioramas
I have come to sorcerous foretelling
        through the eyes of a sickened foetus
through the heat that rises from tainted Mustang skin

I witness
aloof collusional embryonics
where all birth is stained
all naturally corrupted on the visible plane
within its co-agitated penumbra
evolved through anatomical struggle
        through sidereal devolvement
through an unseasoned forte
neutered
which eclipses itself through cause & counter-cause
through movement which endures
        through in-felicitous movement
less & less
as it focuses its breath on the molecules of Sapiens Sapiens

& this is not to say
that Sapiens Sapiens have no right
have no display as to variety or significance

no

I do not degrade human utterance
as sudden neural lessening

yet
my present shape of voice
is magically tangled with single holocaust threading
with nullification being its vatic

as its molecules transmute
I am the bird from magical under-vapour moving
        as jeopardous flask
teleporting my rays to Swedish lakes
to algal congestion in Venice lagoons
        partaking of crucial ozone scintilla
so as to desperately re-surge as ozone across operant duration
3 billion years in the making

not that I am suspicious of new waking
        but I know my power of impact
its garrulous outer task
in a kingdom now sweltering with deformity

my voice
not simply a gloomy didactic
spawned in dark medicinal poisons
but a proto-supernal complexity analogous in human endeavour
        to Moorish Córdoba
with its intensive madrasas
its botany
its medicine
its velocity of percipience

I can be called a mysterious indigo sigil focused as primeval number
upon dark tarantula grasses
unleashing a curious metropolis of galaxies

there exists
Alnilam
Mirfak
Alhena
splayed across the heavens as pure vibrational ciphers
as Andalusian sigils
as crucibles of transparency
there is the binary Hadar
condensed in Iberia
that projects 'etheric shift...allowing being to vary
    its dimensional forms

I as bird
of numerous dimensional shifts
telepathically whirring
as power through alchemical absentia
    being an infiltration of spectres
simultaneous across differing forms voracious
in Sri Lankan mangrove swamps dispersing hells
    in various depths of the Naktong River
disrupting carbonized waste from the Rio de la Plata

perhaps
while fluttering across ravines of hell
    motions from Andromeda will call me
as an ancient miraculous raptor dialectically chronicled
    as blazeless wavering on Earth
juggling death as amorphic delay
my wings encoded with prayer
amidst a battle kaleidoscopic with the gravid
then suddenly re-existing in the Hercules Cluster
aligning my light with the beyond
with the Magellanic Clouds
with Tucana
with the Pinwheel Galaxy focused in Triangulum

a bird who creates a new treatise on voids
never pertaining to soured gargantuan basins
or by sleep unstructured by old insomnial fires

me
the fluidic beast
suddenly spawned out of death
suddenly spawned from invisible guidance
so as to absorb unexplained poisons sleeping in the cracks of
the Earth

because I have been to the sky
& evolved through apostolic ice
I am marked by deciduous flooding
an electrically blank witness
more mystically coiled than an arid Martian cobra
whispering Olmec writing at Carthage then predicting my example with a heliotropic acoustic
so that emptiness appears
being movement from black ocean trenches

perhaps I can swear by ecologic food
or slain fragments of gold

yet I hover
between illusion & that which dazzles itself as omega

because
eclectics persists as horizontal layers exploded out of time

me
traces of vatic lava
fumes
pre-biotic with resurrection
again
flitting from the pre-biotic
to avian codes in isolation

& I being specific elixir
who flits across Ceres
who procures incandescent feasts concussive spirals of starlight

& if my body exudes empirical oneirics
it is a skittish theology
a theology that threads & re-threads
its motion as amorphic circles

not the evasive God as the single action consumed by chance
with its angles
with its rivalries
seeking my form as deleterious conversion

without dialectic formed from one design being resistant to
        culpable cadence as worship
to structured beginnings
to the cells as a lesson in morality

in this one proportional God
one finds
a transcendental salt without mixture
        without blissful mothering wave
sans boundless variety or spectrum

take a sea of tigers
burning as acrostics on one prairie

then an ocean
broken away from two oceans

then any continent or channel
or Ordovician template
or a random sum from Jurassic rays plummeted through myopia
        or reefs

do you understand this energy as arc above mountains?

as green or higher colour

as plane of schismatic enrichment?

let me exhale interior vertigo
as if each sea were falling
each millimeter
each droplet
being a crimson body
soured before the end of the Sun

my dialect
transmundane in function
as a link between spirits
being tenacious brooding by wind
by volcano body
part carnivorous
part neutered as to reflex
burning throughout desire
not unlike
the propaganda of centaurs
whistling like a crack
through the black neurology of gases..."

from Exobiology As Goddess

The poet, like the pure mathematician, depends not on descriptive truth, but on conformity to his hypothetical postulates...
—Northrup Frye

Her range

a katabatic ash *

dispersed

across my strange nomadic hearing

alive as bleak metaboling voids

& she is alive inside this bleakness

with her pure acidulous powers

as audic speculation

as a conclave of serpents

as doubled migratory winds

at one time persistent solely to eastern Asia

she is mirage whose aura is wattage

a blue-white glow

with homoseismal lines welling up from her sluices

like earthquake patterns

or a cunning solfatara

creating for my perusal

a flight of inverted demons

then summoning from her sound

a compound of ammonia & gravity

palpable as burning electrical transition

her ciphers condensed

as a compound intransigent species

as Goddess

she floats through sudden methane harbours
angling dust from seas on the moon

revealing herself as Huerta

as pomegranate

as an iceberg calved from glaciers on Uranus

on nights

when the Sun whispers

she emits her form through reflection

as though created from odour

from Hypabyssal Rocks *

her sound

now sunken to the sea bed with all its auroral fires

the impact of her voice

more disturbing than a grammar of blizzards

or a rigid portion of broken tabular mass

the solar concavity then hovering in a voiceless anti-rain

as pointless electrical fuel

its green totalic mist

suddenly synonymous with Solea

with her broken dromedary plantings

with her treasonous infertility

her voice

grafted with perplexities

with ironics hidden in a floating neural vacuum

in inter-galactic hissing warrens

so to announce her full effect

is far beyond treasurous monotony or snow

she remains the dark unastable onus

the black treaty as balance

flying apart & burning

being mirage as congelation

as formless tributary pony

algid

biting

ingenerate

aroused in one zone as an elemental leopard
in another

as reversal of simooms in amber

alive as percussive obsidian shale

as fluid which dwells at the barrier of ether

I call her

the Chaldean seamstress forging hominids from darkness

& from Arabian blue deserts

she emits her tonality through deafness

as perfect fruit acquired through agenda

so that matter does not transpire as her optic sub-rosa

therefore

she generates topography as combative meridians

through storks of drift

through isometric deeds

as if

in the breaking of ice

her voice created bells

created arteries of vapour

suspended

over 3 or 4 terrains

spliced through distance as motion

we interact as presence within presence

as spirit twice its equal in spirit

so that a range of beasts burns between us

perhaps a skua

or a cormorant

or a platypus

perhaps our haggling is a claw that scalds with radiation

with philosophical half-torment

so that we hang from one another

like scattered alkaloid forms

like floating gestural plankton

her void

oblique with transmutation

with molecular half-boundary

so that our substance writhes

between the x-ray at its minimum

& the sound that combines at atmospheric dioxide

I the woven corona of lightning

& she

the scope of ovarian transmission

we combine as a precipice of morals

always obsessed by blank progressive spasmodic

perhaps we are the jungle inside the moon that irradiates Antarctica

perhaps the ghosts from Kerguellan scallops*

like the fire that exists above the Transarctic Mountains

being a singular dweller in these boiling tectonics

I can say

that her biology projects from a typographic haze

esoteric

& minus the forms eastern Antarctica

an unrivalled domination

as her glare

now a spinning optic krill

now a clashing dialectic of apogees...

Glossary

katabatic ash- A night wind "caused by the flow of air, cooled by radiation, down mountain slopes and valleys."

Hypabyssal Rocks- "Those igneous rocks which have risen towards the earth's surface, but have failed to reach it..."

www.ingramcontent.com/pod-product-compliance
Lightning Source LLC
Chambersburg PA
CBHW051700040426
42446CB00009B/1230